I0901904

FEATHERED FRIENDS

BLUE JAYS

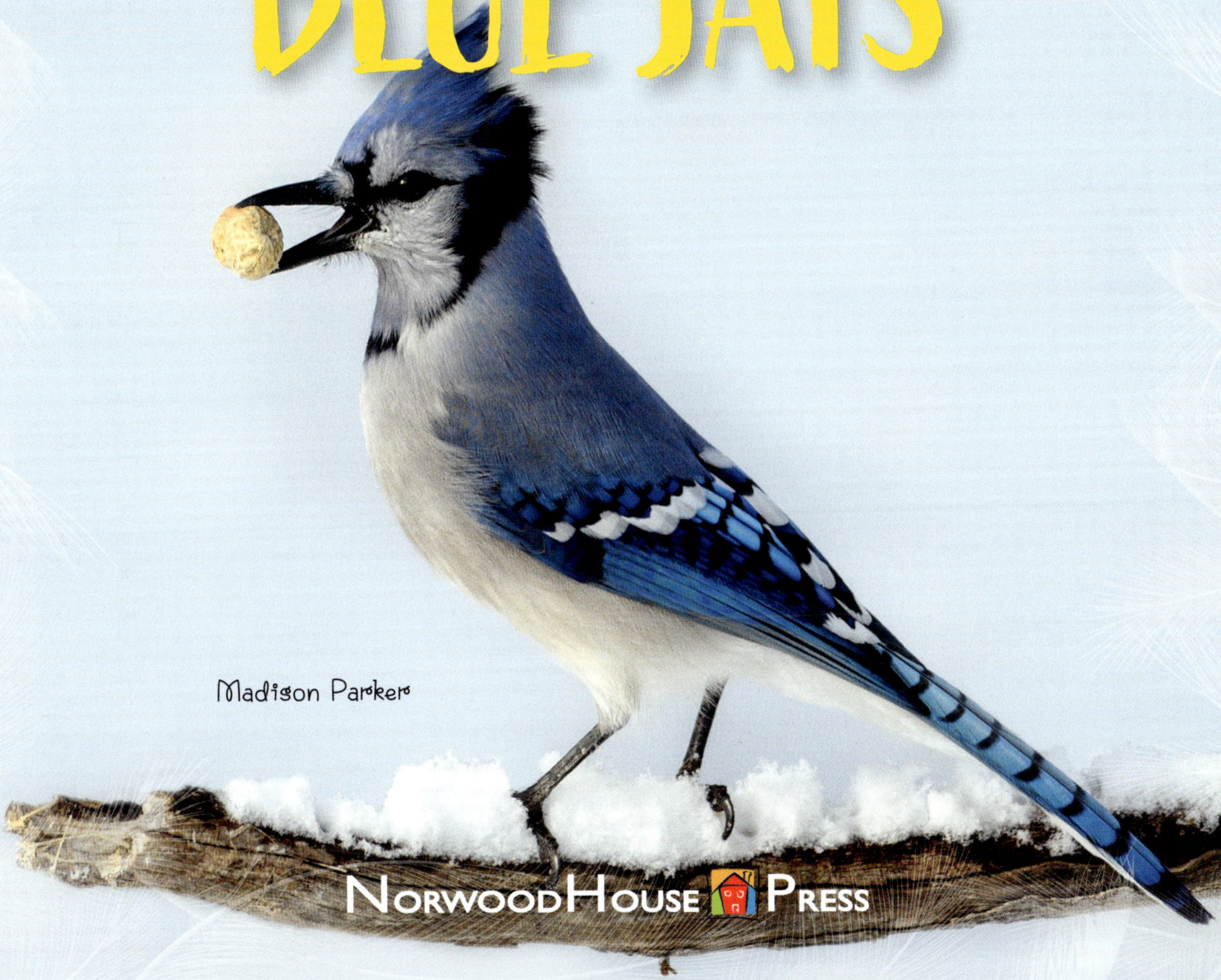

Madison Parker

NorwoodHouse Press

Library of Congress Cataloging-in-Publication Data:

Names: Parker, Madison.
Title: Blue jays / Madison Parker.
Description: Buffalo, NY : Norwood House Press, 2025. | Series: Feathered friends | Includes glossary and index.
Identifiers: ISBN 9781684502776 (pbk.) | ISBN 9781684502783 (library bound) | ISBN 9781684502790 (ebook)
Subjects: LCSH: Blue jay--Juvenile literature.
Classification: LCC QL696.P2367 P375 2025 | DDC 598.8'64--dc23

Published in 2025 by
Norwood House Press
2544 Clinton Street
Buffalo, NY 14224

Copyright © 2025 Norwood House Press
Designer: Ocean Books
Editor: Kim Thompson

Photo credits: Cover, p. 1 FotoRequest/Shutterstock.com; p. 5 Mst bilkis Akter/Shutterstock.com; p. 6 Travis Potter/Shutterstock.com; p. 7 Cathy Keiper/Shutterstock.com; p. 9 SAJE/Shutterstock.com; p. 12 Kirklikedi/Shutterstock.com; p. 13 Stacie Acevedo/Shutterstock.com; p. 16 Ami Parikh/Shutterstock.com; p. 17 JarahB/Shutterstock.com; p. 18 DeniseCPagliano/Shutterstock.com; p. 19 Mike Truchon/Shutterstock.com; p. 21 Gordon Magee/Shutterstock.com

All rights reserved. No part of this book may be reproduced in any form without permission in writing from the publisher, except by a reviewer.

Printed in the United States of America

Some of the images in this book illustrate individuals who are models. The depictions do not imply actual situations or events.

CPSIA compliance information: Batch #CW25NHP: For further information contact Norwood House Press at 1-800-237-9932.

Find us on

TABLE OF CONTENTS

What Do Blue Jays Look Like?

Blue jays are our feathered friends. They are very beautiful birds. They have bright blue feathers on their backs and wings.

Blue jays are medium-sized birds. They have strong, black **beaks** and blue tail feathers.

A blue jay's belly is white. Its face is black and white. It has a tall blue **crest** on its head.

Where Do Blue Jays Live?

Blue jays live in the eastern and central parts of North America. They make their home all the way from the southern part of Canada down through Texas and Florida.

Blue jays build nests high up in tall trees. Their nests are made from twigs, grass, and sometimes paper.

How Do Blue Jays Grow Up?

Blue jay eggs are light blue or white with brown spots. Babies **hatch** after about 18 days. Young blue jays learn to fly and find food in just three weeks.

What Do Blue Jays Eat?

Blue jays enjoy eating nuts, seeds, and insects. They use their strong beaks to crack open tough shells.

They also like to **stash** some food away for later. This helps them have food ready for times when they are really hungry.

Blue jays often visit bird feeders to snack on peanuts and sunflower seeds. They grab the food with their feet. Then, they **peck** it open to eat.

What Sounds Do Blue Jays Make?

Blue jays make lots of different sounds. They chirp, whistle, and even scream.

One of their most common calls is a loud "jay, jay!" They use this sound to talk to other blue jays.

Blue jays can also **mimic** the calls of other birds. They sometimes make hawk sounds to scare away **predators**.

Blue jay sounds have different meanings. Some noises help them talk to each other. Others warn about danger. Blue jays get very loud when a predator is nearby.

What Funny Things Can Blue Jays Do?

Blue jays splash when they take baths. They play by dropping sticks and catching them. Sometimes, they **steal** shiny things like coins and jewelry.

GLOSSARY

beaks (beeks): horny, pointed jaws on birds; bird bills

crest (krest): a tuft of feathers on the top of a bird's head

hatch (hach): to break out of an egg to be born

mimic (MIM-ik): to imitate or copy

peck (pek): to strike something or pick something up with the beak

predators (PRED-uh-turz): animals that live by hunting other animals for food

stash (stash): to hide something away for later use, usually in a secret place

steal (steel): to take something that does not belong to you, especially in secret or by force

THINKING QUESTIONS

1. What does a blue jay look like?

2. What is special about the sounds a blue jay makes?

3. How does a blue jay show it is smart?

4. What do blue jays eat?

5. Why do you think a blue jay is a feathered friend?

INDEX

ABOUT THE AUTHOR

Madison Parker spent her childhood in the city of Chicago, Illinois. A farm girl at heart, today she lives in Wisconsin with her husband and four children on a small farm with cows, goats, chickens, and two miniature horses named Harley and David. Her favorite dessert is vanilla frozen custard with rainbow sprinkles, even in the winter.